The Complete BBQ Cookbook For Beginners

The Complete Guide With Quick And Easy Outdoor Cooking Recipes To Make Your Super Tasty Dishes

Kevin Parker

Disclaimer Notice:

Table of Content

Introduction

Thank you for purchasing **The Complete BBQ Cookbook For Beginners: The Complete Guide With Quick And Easy Outdoor Cooking Recipes To Make Your Super Tasty Dishes**

This culinary technique is nothing else than the evolution of a primitive need of cavemen who realized, despite themselves, that eating dead or killed animals without cooking the meat could be even lethal.

These people were the first ones to cook meat, fish and roots on the fire, experimenting, trying and understanding that by cooking they could obtain a better taste and a more digestible food, in fact this kind of cooking has arrived with some little devices up to now, given by evolution and technology.

Chicken & Beef Recipes

Smoked Chicken Breasts with Dried Herbs

Preparation Time: 15 minutes

Cooking Time: 40 minutes

Servings: 4

Ingredients:

- 4 chicken breasts boneless
- ¼ cup garlic-infused olive oil
- 2 clove garlic minced
- ¼ tsp dried sage
- ¼ tsp dried lavender
- ¼ tsp dried thyme
- ¼ tsp dried mint
- ½ tbsps. dried crushed red pepper
- Kosher salt to taste

Directions:

1. Place the chicken breasts in a shallow plastic container.

2. In a bowl, combine all remaining ingredients, and pour the mixture over the chicken breast and refrigerate for one hour.

3. Remove the chicken breast from the sauce (reserve sauce) and pat dry on kitchen paper.

4. Start your traeger grill on SMOKE (hickory traeger) with the lid open until the fire is established). Set the temperature to 250°F and preheat for 10 to 15 minutes.

5. Place chicken breasts on the smoker. Close traeger grill lid and cook for about 30 to 40 minutes or until chicken breasts reach 165°F.

6. Serve hot with reserved marinade.

Nutrition:

- Calories: 391
- Carbs: 0.7g
- Fat: 3.21g
- Fiber: 0.12g
- Protein: 20.25g

Chicken Enchiladas

Preparation Time: 15 minutes

Cooking Time: 45 minutes

Servings: 6

Ingredients:

- 2 pounds shredded chicken
- 1 tbsp. olive oil
- ½ tbsp. taco seasoning
- 1 tsp. salt
- 1 tsp. onion powder
- 1 tsp. ground black pepper
- ½ tsp. garlic powder
- 1 can (28 ounces) enchilada sauce
- 1 onion (diced)
- 2 cups Mexican blend shredded cheese
- 8 large flour tortilla
- 1 cup sour cream
- 1 (7 ounces) diced green chili

- 2 tbsp. cilantro (chopped)

Directions:

1. In a large mixing bowl, combine the shredded chicken, sour cream, onion, 1 cup shredded cheese, green chilies, onion powder, taco seasoning, pepper, garlic powder.
2. Spoon an equal amount of the chicken mixture into each tortilla and roll.
3. Arrange the stuffed tortilla into a 9-inch by 13-inch greased baking pan.
4. Pour the enchilada sauce over the tortilla and top with the remaining 1 cup cheese. Cover the pan tightly with aluminum foil.
5. Preheat your grill to 350°F with the lid closed for 15 minutes, using mesquite hard traegers.
6. Place the pan on the grill and cook for 30 minutes.
7. Uncover the pan and cook for an additional 1 hour.
8. Remove pan from heat, let the enchilada rest for a few minutes.
9. Cut into sizes. Serve and garnish with chopped cilantro.

Nutrition:

- Calories: 546
- Fat 25.3g
- Carbs: 22.6g
- Fiber: 2.6g
- Protein: 55.2g

Beef Stuffed Bell Peppers

Preparation Time: 20 minutes

Cooking Time: 1 hour

Servings: 6

Ingredients:

- 6 large bell peppers
- 1 pound ground beef
- 1 small onion, chopped
- 2 garlic cloves, minced
- 2 cups cooked rice
- 1 cup frozen corn, thawed
- 1 cup cooked black beans
- 2⁄3 cup salsa
- 2 tbsp. Cajun rub
- 1½ cups Monterey Jack cheese, grated

Directions:

1. Cut each bell pepper in half lengthwise through the stem.

2. Carefully, remove the seeds and ribs.

3. For stuffing: heat a large frying pan and cook the beef for about 6-7 minutes or until browned completely.

4. Add onion and garlic and cook for about 2-3 minutes.

5. Stir in remaining ingredients except for cheese and cook for about 5 minutes.

6. Remove from the heat and set aside to cool slightly.

7. Preheat the Z Grills Traeger Grill & Smoker on grill setting to 350°F.

8. Stuff each bell pepper half with stuffing mixture evenly.

9. Arrange the peppers onto grill, stuffing side up, and cook for about 40 minutes.

10. Sprinkle each bell pepper half with cheese and cook for about 5 minutes more.

11. Remove the bell peppers from grill and serve hot.

Nutrition:

- Calories: 675
- Fat: 14.8 g

- Saturated Fat: 7.5 g
- Cholesterol: 93 mg
- Sodium: 1167 mg
- Carbs: 90.7 g
- Fiber: 8.7 g
- Sugar: 9.1 g
- Protein: 43.9 g

Whole Orange Chicken

Preparation Time: 15 minutes + marinate time

Cooking Time: 45 minutes

Servings: 4

Ingredients:

- 1 whole chicken, 3–4 pounds' backbone removed
- 2 oranges
- ¼ cup oil
- 2 tsp. Dijon mustard
- 1 orange, zest
- 2 tbsp. rosemary leaves, chopped
- 2 tsp. salt

Directions:

1. Clean and pat your chicken dry
2. Take a bowl and mix in orange juice, oil, orange zest, salt, rosemary leaves, Dijon mustard and mix well
3. Marinade chicken for 2 hours or overnight

4. Pre-heat your grill to 350°F

5. Transfer your chicken to the smoker and smoke for 30 minutes' skin down. Flip and smoke until the internal temperature reaches 175°F in the thigh and 165°F in the breast

6. Rest for 10 minutes and carve

7. Enjoy!

Nutrition: Calories: 290 Fats: 15g Carbs: 20g Fiber: 1g

2. Special Occasion's Dinner Cornish Hen

Preparation Time: 15 minutes

Cooking Time: 1 hour

Servings: 4

Ingredients:

- 4 Cornish game hens
- 4 fresh rosemary sprigs
- 4 tbsp. butter, melted
- 4 tsp. chicken rub

Directions:

1. Set the temperature of Grill to 375°F and preheat with closed lid for 15 mins.

2. With paper towels, pat dry the hens.

3. Tuck the wings behind the backs and with kitchen strings, tie the legs together.

4. Coat the outside of each hen with melted butter and sprinkle with rub evenly.

5. Stuff each hen with a rosemary sprig.

6. Place the hens onto the grill and cook for about 50-60 mins.

7. Remove the hens from grill and place onto a platter for about 10 mins.

8. Cut each hen into desired-sized pieces and serve.

Nutrition: Calories: 430 Carbs: 2.1g Protein: 25.4g Fat: 33g Sugar: 0g Sodium: 331mg Fiber: 0.7g

BBQ Breakfast Grist

Preparation Time: 20 minutes

Cooking Time: 30 to 40 minutes

Servings: 8

Ingredients:

- 1 cup water
- 1 cup quick-cooking grits
- 3 tbsp. unsalted butter
- 2 tbsp. minced garlic
- 1 medium onion, chopped
- 1 jalapeño pepper, stemmed, seeded, and chopped
- 1 tsp. cayenne pepper
- 2 tsp. red pepper flakes
- 1 tbsp. hot sauce
- 1 cup shredded Monterey Jack cheese
- 1 cup sour cream
- Salt
- Freshly ground black pepper
- 2 eggs, beaten
- ⅓ cup half-and-half

- 3 cups leftover pulled pork (preferably smoked)

Directions:

1. Supply your smoker with traeger and follow the manufacturer's specific start-up procedure. Preheat, with the lid, closed, to 350°F.
2. On your kitchen stovetop, in a large saucepan over high heat, bring the chicken stock and water to a boil.
3. Add the grits and reduce the heat to low, then stir in the butter, garlic, onion, jalapeño, cayenne, red pepper flakes, hot sauce, cheese, and sour cream. Season with salt and pepper, then cook for about 5 minutes.
4. Temper the beaten eggs and incorporate them into the grits. Remove the saucepan from the heat and stir in the half-and-half and pulled pork.
5. Pour the grits into a greased grill-safe 9-by-13-inch casserole dish or aluminum pan.
6. Transfer to the grill, close the lid, and bake for 30 to 40 minutes, covering with aluminum foil toward the end of cooking if the grits start to get too brown on top.

Nutrition:

- Calories: 1263
- Protein: 36.9g
- Carbs: 110.3g
- Fat: 76.8g
- Sugar: 107g

BBQ Meatloaf

Preparation Time: 20 minutes

Cooking Time: 2½ hours

Servings: 8

Ingredients:

For Meatloaf:

- 3 pounds ground beef
- 3 eggs
- ½ cup panko breadcrumbs
- 1 (10-ounce) can diced tomatoes with green chile

peppers

- 1 large white onion, chopped
- 2 hot banana peppers, chopped
- 2 tbsp. seasoned salt
- 2 tsp. liquid smoke flavoring
- 2 tsp. smoked paprika
- 1 tsp. onion salt
- 1 tsp. garlic salt
- Salt and ground black pepper, as required

For Sauce:

- ½ cup ketchup
- ¼ cup tomato-based chile sauce
- ¼ cup white Sugar:
- 2 tsp. Worcestershire sauce
- 2 tsp. hot pepper sauce
- 1 tsp. red pepper flakes, crushed
- 1 tsp. red chili pepper
- Salt and ground black pepper, as required

Directions:

1. Preheat the Z Grills Traeger Grill & Smoker on smoke setting to 225°F, using charcoal.
2. Grease a loaf pan.
3. For the meatloaf: in a bowl, add all ingredients, and with your hands, mix until well combined.
4. Place the mixture into the prepared loaf pan evenly.
5. Place the pan onto the grill and cook for about 2 hours.
6. For the sauce: in a bowl, add all ingredients and beat until well combined.
7. Remove the pan from the grill and drain excess grease from the meatloaf.

8. Place sauce over meatloaf evenly and place the pan onto the grill.

9. Cook for about 30 minutes.

10. Remove the meatloaf from the grill and set aside for about 10 minutes before serving.

11. Carefully, invert the meatloaf onto a platter.

12. Cut the meatloaf into desired-sized slices and serve.

Nutrition:

- Calories: 423 Fat: 13 g
- Saturated Fat: 4.7 g Cholesterol: 213 mg
- Sodium: 1879 mg Carbs: 15.7 g
- Fiber: 1.5 g
- Sugar: 12.3 g
- Protein: 54.9 g

Sweet & Spicy Beef Brisket

Preparation Time: 10 minutes

Cooking Time: 7 hours

Servings: 10

Ingredients:

- 1 cup paprika
- ¾ cup Sugar:
- 3 tbsp. garlic salt
- 3 tbsp. onion powder
- 1 tbsp. celery salt
- 1 tbsp. lemon pepper
- 1 tbsp. ground black pepper
- 1 tsp. cayenne pepper
- 1 tsp. mustard powder
- ½ tsp. dried thyme, crushed
- 1 (5-6-pound) beef brisket, trimmed

Directions:

1. In a bowl, place all ingredients except for beef brisket and mix well.
2. Rub the brisket with spice mixture generously.

3. With plastic wrap, cover the brisket and refrigerate overnight.

4. Preheat the Z Grills Traeger Grill & Smoker on grill setting to 250°F.

5. Place the brisket onto grill over indirect heat and cook for about 3–3½ hours.

6. Flip and cook for about 3–3½ hours more.

7. Remove the brisket from grill and place onto a cutting board for about 10-15 minutes before slicing.

8. With a sharp knife, cut the brisket into desired sized slices and serve.

Nutrition:

- Calories: 536
- Fat: 15.6 g
- Saturated Fat: 5.6 g
- Cholesterol: 203 mg
- Sodium: 158 mg
- Carbs: 24.8 g
- Fiber: 4.5 g
- Sugar: 17.4 g

- Protein: 71.1 g

Perfect Smoked Chicken Patties

Preparation Time: 20 minutes

Cooking Time: 50 minutes

Servings: 6

Ingredients:

- 2 lb. ground chicken breast
- 2⁄3 cup minced onion
- 1 tbsps. cilantro (chopped)
- 2 tbsp. fresh parsley, finely chopped
- 2 tbsp. olive oil
- ⅛ tsp crushed red pepper flakes
- ½ tsp ground cumin
- 2 tbsps. fresh lemon juice
- 3⁄4 tsp kosher salt
- 2 tsp paprika
- Hamburger buns for serving

Directions:

1. In a bowl combine all ingredients from the list.

2. Using your hands, mix well. Form mixture into 6 patties. Refrigerate until ready to grill (about 30 minutes).

3. Start your traeger grill on SMOKE with the lid open until the fire is established). Set the temperature to 350°F and preheat for 10 to 15 minutes.

4. Arrange chicken patties on the grill rack and cook for 35 to 40 minutes turning once.

5. Serve hot with hamburger buns and your favorite condiments.

Nutrition:

- Calories: 258
- Carbs: 2.5g
- Fat: 9.4g
- Fiber: 0.6g
- Protein: 39g

Crispy & Juicy Chicken

Preparation Time: 15 minutes

Cooking Time: 5 hours Servings: 6

Ingredients:

- ¾ cup. dark brown sugar:
- ½ cup. ground espresso beans
- 1 tbsp. ground cumin
- 1 tbsp. ground cinnamon
- 1 tbsp. garlic powder
- 1 tbsp. cayenne pepper
- Salt and ground black pepper, to taste
- 1 (4-lb.) whole chicken, neck and giblets removed

Directions:

1. Set the temperature of Grill to 200-225°F and preheat with closed lid for 15 mins.
2. In a bowl, mix together brown sugar, ground espresso, spices, salt and black pepper.
3. Rub the chicken with spice mixture generously.
4. Put the chicken onto the grill and cook for about 3-5 hours.

5. Remove chicken from grill and place onto a cutting board for about 10 mins before carving.

6. Cut the chicken into desired sized pieces and serve.

Nutrition: Calories: 540 Carbs: 20.7g Protein: 88.3g Fat: 9.6g Sugar: 18.1g Sodium: 226mg Fiber: 1.2g

Brandy Beef Tenderloin

Preparation Time: 15 minutes

Cooking Time: 2 hours 2 minutes

Servings: 6

Ingredients:

For Brandy Butter:

- ½ cup butter
- 1 ounce brandy

For Brandy Sauce:

- 2 ounces brandy
- 8 garlic cloves, minced
- ¼ cup mixed fresh herbs (parsley, rosemary and thyme), chopped
- 2 tsp. honey
- 2 tsp. hot English mustard

For Tenderloin:

- 1 (2-pound) center-cut beef tenderloin
- Salt and cracked black peppercorns, as required

Directions:

1. Preheat the Z Grills Traeger Grill & Smoker on grill setting to 230°F.

2. For brandy butter: in a pan, melt butter over medium-low heat.

3. Stir in brandy and remove from heat.

4. Set aside, covered to keep warm.

5. For brandy sauce: in a bowl, add all ingredients and mix until well combined.

6. Season the tenderloin with salt and black peppercorns generously.

7. Coat tenderloin with brandy sauce evenly.

8. With a baster-injector, inject tenderloin with brandy butter.

9. Place the tenderloin onto the grill and cook for about ½–2 hours, injecting with brandy butter occasionally.

10. Remove the tenderloin from grill and place onto a cutting board for about 10–15 minutes before serving.

11. With a sharp knife, cut the tenderloin into desired-sized slices and serve.

Nutrition:

- Calories: 496
- Fat: 29.3 g
- Saturated Fat: 15 g
- Cholesterol: 180 mg
- Sodium: 240 mg
- Carbs: 4.4 g
- Fiber: 0.7 g
- Sugar: 2 g
- Protein: 44.4 g

Porchetta

Preparation Time: 30 minutes

Cook time: 3 hours

Servings: 12

Ingredients:

- 6 pounds' skin-on pork belly
- 4 pounds' center-cut pork loin
- 4 tbsp. olive oil
- 1 cup apple juice
- 2 garlic cloves, minced
- 1 onion, diced
- 1 ¼ cups grated pecorino Romano cheese
- 1 tsp ground black pepper
- 2 tsp. kosher salt
- 3 tbsp. fennel seeds
- 1 tbsp. freshly chopped rosemary
- 1 tbsp. freshly chopped sage
- 1 tbsp. freshly chopped thyme
- 1 tbsp. grated lemon zest

Rub:

- 1 tbsp. chili powder
- 2 tsp. grilling seasoning
- 1 tsp. salt or to taste
- ½ tsp. cayenne
- 1 tsp. oregano
- 1 tsp. paprika
- 1 tsp. mustard powder

Directions:

1. Butterfly the pork loin and place it in the middle of two plastic wraps. On a flat surface, pound the pork evenly until it is ½ inch thick.
2. Combine all the rub ingredients in a small mixing bowl.
3. Place the butterflied pork on a flat surface, cut side up. Season the cut side generously with ⅓ of the rub.
4. Heat 1 tbsp. olive oil in a frying pan over medium to high heat. Add the onion, garlic, and fennel seed. Sauté until the veggies are tender.
5. Stir the black pepper, 1 tsp. kosher salt, rosemary, sage, thyme, and lemon zest. Cook for 1 minute and stir in the cheese.

6. Put the sautéed ingredients on the flat pork and spread evenly. Roll up the pork like you are rolling a burrito.

7. Brush the rolled pork loin with 1 tbsp. oil and season with the remaining rub. The loin with butcher's string at the 1-inch interval.

8. Roll the pork belly around the pork, skin side out. Brush the pork belly with the remaining oil and season with 1 tsp. salt.

9. Set a rack into a roasting pan and place the Porchetta on the rack. Pour the wine into the bottom of the roasting pan.

10. Start your grill on smoke mode, leaving the lid opened for 5 minutes until the fire starts.

11. Close the lid and preheat the grill to 325°F, using maple or apple hard pellets.

12. Place the roasting pan on the grill and roast Porchetta for about 3 hours or until the Porchetta's internal temperature reaches 155°F.

13. Remove the Porchetta from heat and let it rest for a few minutes to cool.

14. Remove the butcher's string. Slice Porchetta into sizes and serve.

Nutrition:

- Calories: 611
- Fat: 22.7g
- Cholesterol: 252mg
- Carbohydrate: 6.6g
- Protein: 89.4g

Blackened Steak

Preparation Time: 10 minutes

Cooking Time: 60 minutes

Servings: 4

Ingredients:

- 2 steaks, about 40 ounces each
- 4 tbsp. blackened rub
- 4 tbsp. butter, unsalted

Directions:

1. Switch on the Traeger grill, fill the grill hopper with hickory flavored traegers, power the grill on by using the control panel, select 'smoke' on the temperature dial, or set the temperature to 225°F and let it preheat for a minimum of 15 minutes.
2. Transfer steaks to a dish and then repeat with the remaining steak.
3. Let seared steaks rest for 10 minutes, then slice each steak across the grain and serve.

Nutrition:

- Calories: 184.4

- Fat: 8.8 g
- Carbs: 0 g
- Protein: 23.5 g

Hearty Pig Candies

Preparation Time: 20 minutes Cooking Time: 2 hours

Servings: 10

Ingredients:

- Nonstick cooking spray
- 2 pound bacon slices
- 1 cup firmly packed brown sugar
- 2-3 tsp. cayenne pepper
- ½ a cup maple syrup

Directions:

1. Take your drip pan and add water; cover with aluminum foil. Pre-heat your smoker to 225°F
2. Use water fill water pan halfway through and place it over drip pan. Add wood chips to the side tray Remove the grill rack from your smoker and cover with aluminum foil; spray the foils with cooking spay Lay the bacon in a single layer, making sure to leave a bit of space in between Take a small bowl and add brown sugar, cayenne, and mix Baste the bacon with ¼ cup of maple syrup Sprinkle half of the rub on top of the bacon

3. Transfer the rack to the smoker alongside the bacon and smoke for 1 hour Flip the bacon and baste with another ¼ cup of maple syrup, sprinkle more rub, and a smoker for 1 hour more Once the bacon is brown and firm, it's ready to be served!

Nutrition:Calories: 152 Fats: 10g Carbs: 13g Fiber: 2g

Grilled Steak with American Cheese Sandwich

Preparation Time: 10 minutes

Cooking Time: 55 minutes

Servings: 4

Ingredients:

- 1 pound beef steak.
- ½ tsp. salt to taste.
- ½ tsp. pepper to taste.
- 1 tbsp. Worcestershire sauce.
- 2 tbsp. butter.
- 1 chopped onion.
- ½ chopped green bell pepper.
- Salt and pepper to taste.
- 8 slices American Cheese
- 8 slices white bread.
- 4 tbsp. butter.

Directions:

1. Turn your Traeger Smoker and Grill to smoke and fire up for about four to five minutes. Set the temperature of the

grill to 450°F and let it preheat for about ten to fifteen minutes with its lid closed.

2. Next, place a non-stick skillet on the griddle and preheat for about fifteen minutes until it becomes hot. Once hot, add in the butter and let melt. Once the butter melts, add in the onions and green bell pepper then cook for about five minutes until they become brown in color, set aside.

3. Next, still using the same pan on the griddle, add in the steak, Worcestershire sauce, salt, and pepper to taste then cook for about five to six minutes until it is cooked through. Add in the cooked bell pepper mixture; stir to combine then heat for another three minutes, set aside.

4. Use a sharp knife to slice the bread in half, butter each side then grill for about three to four minutes with its sides down. To assemble, add slices of cheese on each bread slice, top with the steak mixture then your favorite toppings, close the sandwich with another bread slice then serve.

Nutrition:

- Calories: 589
- Carbs: 28g

- Protein: 24g
- Fat: 41g
- Fiber: 2g

BBQ Brisket

Preparation Time: 12 hours

Cooking Time: 10 hours

Servings: 8

Ingredients:

- 1 beef brisket, about 12 pounds
- Beef rub as needed

Directions:

1. Season beef brisket with beef rub until well coated, place it in a large plastic bag, seal it and let it marinate for a minimum of 12 hours in the refrigerator.

2. When ready to cook, switch on the Traeger grill, fill the grill hopper with hickory flavored traegers, power the grill on by using the control panel, select 'smoke' on the temperature dial, or set the temperature to 225°F and let it preheat for a minimum of 15 minutes. When the grill has preheated, open the lid, place marinated brisket on the grill grate fat-side down, shut the grill, and smoke for 6 hours until the internal temperature reaches 160°F. Then wrap the brisket in foil,

return it back to the grill grate and cook for 4 hours until the internal temperature reaches 204°F.

3. When done, transfer brisket to a cutting board, let it rest for 30 minutes, then cut it into slices and serve.

Nutrition: Calories: 328 Fat: 21 g Protein: 32 g

Guinea Fowl Stuffed with Vegetables

Preparation Time: 10 minutes

Cooking Time: 2 hours

Servings: 5

Ingredients:

- 1 guinea fowl
- 2 shallots
- 13 cloves garlic
- 20 g parsley
- Salt
- Olive oil
- 10 onions cut into quarters
- 5 large potatoes cut into quarters
- 3 pickled tomatoes
- 4 fresh or canned tomatoes (skinless and cut into quarters)
- Fresh thyme
- 200 g chicken broth or broth from any other poultry
- 20-30 g butter
- Ground black pepper

Directions:

1. Stuff the guinea fowl with 2 shallots, 3 cloves of garlic, a slice of butter, thyme, and chopped parsley. Outside, pepper and salt the guinea fowl.
2. Put the stuffed guinea fowl in a cast-iron roaster and fry on all sides in a large amount of olive oil. After that, take out the guinea fowl from the roaster and put it aside temporarily, and fry the potatoes, onions, and garlic cloves in olive oil. Add chopped tomatoes (both) to vegetables. Put the thyme, salt, and ground pepper here. Pour in 100 g of broth. Place the guinea fowl on a layer of vegetables.
3. Place the roaster in an oven preheated to 170°. Keep the guinea fowl there for 75 minutes. Moreover, every 15 minutes it is necessary to water the guinea fowl from above with the remaining broth.

Nutrition:

- Calories: 157
- Fat: 18g
- Carbs: 17g
- Fiber: 1.3 g

- Protein: 15.1g

Pig Pops (Sweet-hot Bacon on Stick)

Preparation Time: 15 minutes

Cooking Time: 25 to 30 minutes

Servings: 24

Ingredients:

- Nonstick cooking spray, oil, or butter, for greasing
- 2 pounds thick-cut bacon (24 slices)
- 24 metal skewers
- 1 cup packed light brown sugar:
- 2 to 3 tsp. cayenne pepper
- ½ cup maple syrup, divided

Directions:

1. Supply your smoker with traeger and follow the manufacturer's specific start-up procedure. Preheat, with the lid, closed, to 350°F.
2. Coat a disposable aluminum foil baking sheet with cooking spray, oil, or butter.

3. Thread each bacon slice onto a metal skewer and place on the prepared baking sheet.

4. In a medium bowl, stir together the brown Sugar: and cayenne.

5. Baste the top sides of the bacon with ¼ cup of maple syrup.

6. Sprinkle half of the brown Sugar: mixture over the bacon

7. Place the baking sheet on the grill, close the lid, and smoke for 15 to 30 minutes.

8. Using tongs, flip the bacon skewers. Baste with the remaining ¼ cup of maple syrup and top with the remaining brown Sugar: mixture.

9. Continue smoking with the lid closed for 10 to 15 minutes, or until crispy. You can eyeball the bacon and smoke to your desired doneness, but the actual ideal internal temperature for bacon is 155°F (if you want to try to get a thermometer into it—ha!).

10. Using tongs, carefully remove the bacon skewers from the grill. Let cool completely before handling.

Nutrition:

- Calories: 318
- Carbs: 7g
- Fat: 10g
- Protein: 8g

Maple Turkey Breast

Preparation Time: 4 hours and 30 minutes

Cooking Time: 2 hours

Servings: 4

Ingredients:

- 3 tbsp. olive oil
- 3 tbsp. dark brown sugar:
- 3 tbsp. garlic, minced
- 2 tbsp. Cajun seasoning
- 2 tbsp. Worcestershire sauce
- 6 lb. turkey breast fillets

Directions:

1. Combine olive oil, sugar, garlic, Cajun seasoning, and Worcestershire sauce in a bowl.
2. Soak the turkey breast fillets in the marinade.
3. Cover and marinate for 4 hours.
4. Grill the turkey at 180°F for 2 hours.

Serving suggestion: Let rest for 15 minutes before serving.

Preparation / Cooking Tips: You can also sprinkle dry rub on the turkey before grilling.

Nutrition:

- Calories: 416 Fat: 13.3 g
- Carbs: 0 g Protein: 69.8 g
- Fiber: 0 g

Trager Smoked Spatchcock Turkey

Preparation Time: 30 minutes

Cooking Time: 1 hour 15 minutes

Servings: 8

Ingredients:

- turkey
- ½ cup melted butter
- 1/4 cup Traeger chicken rub
- 1 tbsp. onion powder
- 1 tbsp. garlic powder
- 1 tbsp. rubbed sage

Directions:

1. Preheat your Traeger to high temperature.

2. Place the turkey on a chopping board with the breast side down and the legs pointing towards you.

3. Cut either side of the turkey backbone, to remove the spine. Flip the turkey and place it on a pan

4. Season both sides with the seasonings and place it on the grill skin side up on the grill.

5. Cook for 30 minutes, reduce temperature, and cook for 45 more minutes or until the internal temperature reaches 165°F. Remove from the Traeger and let rest for 15 minutes before slicing and serving.

Nutrition:Calories: 156 Fat: 16g Protein: 2g Fiber: 0g Sodium: 19mg

Party Pulled Pork Shoulder

Preparation Time: 30 minutes

Cooking Time: 8 to 9 minutes

Servings: 10

Ingredients:

- 1 (5-pound) Boston butt (pork shoulder)
- ¼ cup prepared table mustard
- ½ cup Our House Dry Rub or your favorite rub, divided
- 2 cups apple juice
- ½ cup of salt

Directions:

1. Slather the meat with the mustard and coat with ¼ cup of the dry rub.
2. In a spray bottle, mix the apple juice and salt and shake until the salt is dissolved.
3. Supply your smoker with a traeger and follow the manufacturer's specific start-up procedure. Preheat, with the lid, closed, to 225°F.
4. Place the pork fat-side up in an aluminum pan, transfer to the grill, close the lid, and smoke for 8 to 9 hours, spritzing

well all over with the salted apple juice every hour, until a meat thermometer inserted in the thickest part of the meat reads 205°F. Cover the pork loosely with aluminum foil toward the end of cooking, if necessary, to keep the top from blackening.

5. Drain the liquid from the pan, cover, and allow the meat to cool for a few minutes before using two forks to shred it.

6. Sprinkle the remaining rub over the meat and serve with barbecue sauce.

Nutrition:

- Calories: 426;
- Protein: 65.3g;
- Carbs: 20.4g;
- Fat: 8.4g
- Sugar: 17.8g

Sauced Up Pork Spares

Preparation Time: 5 hours

Cooking Time: 4 hours

Serving: 6

Ingredients:

- 6 pound pork spareribs

For Dry Rub

- ½ cup packed brown sugar:
- 2 tbsp. chili powder
- 1 tbsp. paprika
- 1 tbsp. freshly ground black pepper
- 2 tbsp. garlic powder
- 2 tsp. onion powder
- 2 tsp. kosher salt
- 2 tsp. ground cumin
- 1 tsp. ground cinnamon
- 1 tsp. jalapeno seasoning salt
- 1 tsp. Cayenne pepper

For Mop Sauce

- 1 cup apple cider

- ¾ cup apple cider vinegar
- 1 tbsp. onion powder
- 1 tbsp. garlic powder
- 2 tbsp. lemon juice
- 1 jalapeno pepper, chopped
- 3 tbsp. hot pepper sauce
- Kosher salt as needed
- Black pepper as needed
- 2 cups soaked wood chips

Directions:

1. Take a medium-sized bowl and add brown sugar, chili powder, 2 tbsp. of garlic powder, 2 tsp. of onion powder, cumin, cinnamon, kosher salt, cayenne pepper, jalapeno seasoning
2. Mix well and rub the mixture over the pork spare ribs
3. Allow it to refrigerate for 4 hours
4. Take your drip pan and add water; cover with aluminum foil. Pre-heat your smoker to 225°F
5. Use water fill water pan halfway through and place it over drip pan. Add wood chips to the side tray

6. Take a medium bowl and stir in apple cider, apple cider vinegar, 1 tbsp. of onion powder, jalapeno, 1 tbsp. of garlic powder, salt, pepper, and lemon juice

7. Add a handful of soaked wood chips and transfer the ribs to your smoker middle rack

8. Smoke for 3–4 hours, making sure to keep adding chips after every hour

9. Take the meat out and serve!

Nutrition:

- Calories: 1591 Fats: 120g
- Carbs: 44g
- Fiber: 3g

Lemon Pepper Pork Tenderloin

Preparation Time: 20 minutes

Cooking Time: 20 minutes

Servings: 6

Ingredients:

- 2 pounds’ pork tenderloin, Fat: trimmed

For the Marinade:

- ½ tsp. minced garlic
- 2 lemons, zested
- 1 tsp. minced parsley
- ½ tsp. salt
- ¼ tsp. ground black pepper
- 1 tsp. lemon juice
- 2 tbsp. olive oil

Directions:

1. Prepare the marinade and for this, take a small bowl, place all of its ingredients in it and whisk until combined.
2. Take a large plastic bag, pour marinade in it, add pork tenderloin, seal the bag, turn it upside down to coat the pork,

and let it marinate for a minimum of 2 hours in the refrigerator.

3. When ready to cook, switch on the Traeger grill, fill the grill hopper with apple-flavored pellets, power the grill on by using the control panel, select 'smoke' on the temperature dial, or set the temperature to 375°F and let it preheat for a minimum of 15 minutes.

4. When the grill has preheated, open the lid, place pork tenderloin on the grill grate, shut the grill, and smoke for 20 minutes until the internal temperature reaches 145°F, turning pork halfway.

5. When done, transfer pork to a cutting board, let it rest for 10 minutes, then cut it into slices and serve.

Nutrition:

- Calories: 288.5
- Fat: 16.6 g
- Carbs: 6.2 g
- Protein: 26.4 g
- Fiber: 1.2 g

Wild Turkey Egg Rolls

Preparation Time: 10 minutes

Cooking Time: 55 minutes

Servings: 1

Ingredients:

- ½ cup Corn
- 2 cups Leftover wild turkey meat
- ½ cup Black beans
- 3 tbsp. Taco seasoning
- ½ cup Water
- 1 can Rotel chilies and tomatoes
- 12 Egg roll wrappers
- 4 Cloves minced garlic
- 1 chopped Poblano pepper or 2 jalapeno peppers
- ½ cup Chopped white onion

Directions:

1. Add some olive oil to a fairly large skillet. Heat it over medium heat on a stove.
2. Add peppers and onions. Sauté the mixture for 2–3 minutes until it turns soft.

3. Add some garlic and sauté for another 30 seconds. Add the Rotel chilies and beans to the mixture. Keeping mixing the content gently. Reduce the heat and then simmer.

4. After about 4–5 minutes, pour in the taco seasoning and 1⁄3 cup of water over the meat. Mix everything and coat the meat well. If you feel that it is a bit dry, you can add 2 tbsp. of water. Keep cooking until everything is heated all the way through.

5. Remove the content from the heat and box it to store in a refrigerator. Before you stuff the mixture into the egg wrappers, it should be completely cool to avoid breaking the rolls.

6. Place a spoonful of the cooked mixture in each wrapper and then wrap it securely and tightly. Do the same with all the wrappers.

7. Preheat the traeger grill and brush it with some oil. Cook the egg rolls for 15 minutes on both sides, until the exterior is nice and crispy.

8. Remove them from the grill and enjoy with your favorite salsa!

Nutrition:

- Carbs: 26.1 g
- Protein: 9.2 g
- Fat: 4.2 g
- Sodium: 373.4 mg
- Cholesterol: 19.8 mg

Smoked Turkey

Preparation Time: 1 day and 1 hour

Cooking Time: 4 hours and 30 minutes

Servings: 6

Ingredients:

- 2 gallons of water, divided
- 2 cups sugar
- 2 cups salt
- Ice cubes
- 1 whole turkey
- ½ cup kosher salt
- ½ cup black pepper
- 3 sticks butter, sliced

Directions:

1. Add one-quart water to a pot over medium heat.
2. Stir in the 2 cups each of sugar and salt.
3. Bring to a boil.
4. Remove from heat and let cool.
5. Add ice and the remaining water.
6. Stir to cool.

7. Add the turkey to the brine.

8. Cover and refrigerate for 24 hours.

9. Rinse the turkey and dry with paper towels.

10. Season with salt and pepper.

11. Preheat the Traeger grill to 180°F for 15 minutes while the lid is closed.

12. Smoke the turkey for 2 hours.

13. Increase temperature to 225°F. Smoke for another 1 hour.

14. Increase temperature to 325°F. Smoke for 30 minutes.

15. Place the turkey on top of a foil sheet.

16. Add butter on top of the turkey.

17. Cover the turkey with foil.

18. Reduce temperature to 165°F.

19. Cook on the grill for 1 hour.

Nutrition:

- Calories: 48.2
- Fats: 1.4 g
- Cholesterol: 21.5 mg
- Carbs: 0 g

- Fiber: 0 g
- Sugar: 0 g
- Protein: 8.3 g

All American BBQ Spare Ribs

Preparation Time: 15 minutes Cooking Time: 2 hours

Servings: 8

Ingredients:

- 2 racks grill, 2.75 kg skinned pork ribs
- 2 to 3 tbsp. chicken seasoning
- 1 cup apple juice, cider, or beer
- 50 g barbecue sauce

Directions:

1. Remove the silver skin part on the back of the ribs (Indian I butcher said not yet). Said would prevent the penetration of the herbs and smoke.

2. Sprinkle the chicken seasoning on both sides of the ribs. When you are ready to cook, start the Traeger grill on SMOKE with the lid open until there is a good fire (4 to 5 minutes).

3. Increase the temperature to 95 ° C and preheat with the lid closed for 10 to 15 minutes. Arrange the ribs on the racks or grid, with the bones down. Cook for 3 to 4 hours. After 1 hour, spray with call juice. Repeat said after every hour of cooking. After 3 to 4 hours of cooking, rub the ribs with the barbecue

sauce. Grill for another 30 minutes to 1 hour, cut into individual ribs and serve with extra barbecue sauce.

Nutrition:Calories: 157 Fat: 10g Carbs: 10g Fiber: 1.3 g Protein: 11.1g

Vegetables and Vegetarian Recipes

Smoked Vegetables with Vinaigrette

Preparation Time: 15 minutes Cooking Time: 4 hours

Servings: 4

Ingredients:

- Zucchini (thickly sliced)
- Red potatoes (small in size & chopped)
- Red onions (chopped)
- Yellow medium squash (thickly sliced)
- Red pepper (chopped)

Vinaigrette Ingredients:

- 1/3 cup olive oil
- ¼ cup vinegar (balsamic)
- 2 tsp. Dijon mustard
- Pepper
- Salt

Directions:

1. Add and combine balsamic vinegar, olive oil, Mustard, pepper, and salt in a bowl.
2. In a casserole dish, add all the vegetables and combine. Coat the vegetables with the balsamic vinaigrette by tossing.

3. Preheat your smoker to 225F. Put the dish with the vegetables in the smoker and smoke for 4 hours.

Nutrition: alories: 225 Fat: 17.2g Saturated Fat: 2.5g Carbs: 16.8g Protein: 2.8g Sodium: 196mg Cholesterol: 0mg Calcium: 35mg Potassium: 483mg Iron: 1mg

Sweet Potato Chips

Preparation Time: 10 Minutes

Cooking Time: 12 to 15 Minutes

Servings: 4

Ingredients:

- 2 sweet potatoes
- 1-quart warm water
- 1 tbsp. cornstarch, plus 2 tsp.
- ¼ cup extra-virgin olive oil
- 1 tbsp. salt
- 1 tbsp. packed brown sugar
- 1 tsp. ground cinnamon
- 1 tsp. freshly ground black pepper
- ½ tsp. cayenne pepper

Directions:

1. Using a mandolin, thinly slice the sweet potatoes.
2. Pour the warm water into a large bowl and add 1 tbsp. of cornstarch and the potato slices. Let soak for 15 to 20 minutes.

3. Supply your smoker with Traeger and follow the manufacturer's specific start-up procedure. Preheat, with the lid closed, to 375°F.

4. Drain the potato slices, then arrange in a single layer on a perforated pizza pan or a baking sheet lined with aluminum foil. Brush the potato slices on both sides with olive oil.

5. In a small bowl, whisk together the salt, brown sugar, cinnamon, black pepper, cayenne pepper, and the remaining 2 tsp. of cornstarch. Sprinkle this seasoning blend on both sides of the potatoes.

6. Place the pan or baking sheet on the grill grate, close the lid, and smoke for 35 to 45 minutes, flipping after 20 minutes until the chips curl up and become crispy.

7. Store in an airtight container.

Ingredient Tip:

Avoid storing your sweet potatoes in the refrigerator's produce bin, which tends to give them a hard center and an unpleasant flavor. What, you don't have a root cellar? Just keep them in a cool, dry area of your kitchen.

Nutrition:

- Calories: 150
- Carbs: 15 g
- Protein: 79 g
- Sodium: 45 mg
- Cholesterol: 49 mg

29. Southern Slaw

Preparation Time: 10 Minutes

Cooking Time: 12 to 14 Minutes

Servings: 4

Ingredients:

- 1 head cabbage, shredded
- ¼ cup white vinegar
- ¼ cup sugar
- 1 tsp. paprika
- ½ tsp. salt
- ½ tsp. freshly ground black pepper
- 1 cup heavy (whipping) cream

Directions:

1. Place the shredded cabbage in a large bowl.

2. In a small bowl, combine the vinegar, sugar, paprika, salt, and pepper.

3. Pour the vinegar mixture over the cabbage and mix well.

4. Fold in the heavy cream and refrigerate for at least 1 hour before serving.

Nutrition:

- Calories: 130
- Carbs: 5 g
- Protein: 79 g
- Sodium: 45 mg
- Cholesterol: 19 mg

Fish & Seafood Recipes

Roasted Yellowtail

Preparation Time: 10 minutes

Cooking Time: 30 minutes

Servings: 4

Ingredients:

- 4 Yellowtail Filets (6 oz.)
- 1 lb. new Potatoes
- 2 tbsp. Olive oil
- 1 lb. Mushrooms, oyster
- 1 tsp. ground Black pepper
- 4 tbsp. olive oil

Salsa Verde:

- 1 tbsp. Cilantro, chopped
- 2 tbsp. Mint, chopped
- ½ cup Parsley, chopped
- 2 cloves garlic, minced
- 1 tbsp. Oregano, chopped
- 1 Lemon, the juice
- 1 cup Olive oil
- 1/8 tsp. Pepper Flake

- Salt

Directions:

1. Preheat the grill to high with a closed lid.
2. Place an Iron: pan directly on the grill. Let it heat for 10 minutes.
3. Rub the fish with oil. Season with black pepper and salt.
4. In 2 different bowls place the mushrooms and potatoes, drizzle with oil, and season with black pepper and salt. Toss.
5. Place the potatoes in the pan. Cook 10 minutes. Add the mushrooms.
6. Place the fillets on the grate with the skin down. Cook for 6 minutes and flip. Cook for 4 minutes more.
7. While the potatoes, mushrooms, and fish are cooking make the Salsa Verde. In a bowl combine all the ingredients and stir to combine.
8. Place the mushrooms and potatoes on a plate, top with a fillet, and drizzle with the Salsa Verde.
9. Serve and Enjoy!

Nutrition:

- Calories: 398

- Protein: 52g
- Carbs: 20g
- Fat: 18gg

Grilled Oysters with Tequila Butter

Preparation Time: 20 minutes

Cooking Time: 25 minutes

Servings: 6

Ingredients:

- ½ tsp. fennel seeds
- ¼ tsp. crushed red pepper
- 7 tbsp. unsalted butter
- ¼ cup sage leaves, plus 36 small leaves for the garnish
- 1 tsp. dried oregano
- 2 tbsp. lemon juice
- 2 tbsp. tequila
- Kosher salt
- rock salt, for the serving
- 3 dozen scrubbed medium oysters

Intolerances:

- Gluten-Free
- Egg-Free
- Lactose-Free

Directions:

1. Using a skillet, toast the fennel seeds and squashed red pepper over moderate heat until fragrant for 1 minute.
2. Move onto a mortar and let it cool. With a pestle, pound the spices to a coarse powder, and then move into a bowl.
3. Using the same skillet, cook 3 ½ tbsp. of the butter over moderate heat until it becomes dark-colored, about two minutes.
4. Add ¼ cup of sage and keep cooking, occasionally turning, for about 2 minutes. Move the sage onto a plate.
5. Transfer the butter into the bowl with the spices. Repeat with the remaining butter and sage leaves. Put some aside for decoration.
6. Put the fried sage leaves onto the mortar and squash them with the pestle. Add the squashed sage to the butter along with the oregano, lemon juice, and tequila, and season with salt. Keep warm.
7. Set up the grill. Line a platter with rock salt. Grill the oysters over high heat until they open, about 1 to 2 minutes.
8. Dispose of the top shell and spot the oysters on the rock salt, being careful not to spill their juice.

9. Spoon the warm tequila sauce over the oysters, decorate with a fresh sage leaf, and serve.

Nutrition:

- Calories: 68
- Fat: 3g
- Carbs: 4g
- Protein: 10g

Prosciutto Wrapped Scallops

Preparation Time: 15 minutes

Cooking Time: 40 minutes

Servings: 4

Ingredients:

- 8 large scallops, shelled and cleaned
- 8 extra-thin prosciutto slices

Directions:

1. Preheat the Z Grills Traeger Grill & Smoker on grill setting to 225-250°F.
2. Arrange the prosciutto slices onto a smooth surface.
3. Place 1 scallop on the edge of 1 prosciutto slice and roll it up tucking in the sides of the prosciutto to cover completely.
4. Repeat with remaining scallops and prosciutto slices
5. Arrange the wrapped scallops onto a small wire rack.
6. Place the wire rack onto the grill and cook for about 40 minutes.
7. Remove the scallops from the grill and serve hot.

Nutrition:

- Calories: 160 Fat: 6.7 g

- Saturated Fat: 2.3 g Cholesterol: 64 mg
- Sodium: 1000 mg Carbs: 1.4 g
- Fiber: 0 g Sugar 0 g
- Protein: 23.5 g

Baked Steelhead

Preparation Time: 15 minutes

Cooking Time: 20 minutes

Servings: 4 - 6

Ingredients:

- 1 Lemon
- 2 Garlic cloves, minced
- ½ Shallot, minced
- 3 tbsp. Butter, unsalted
- Saskatchewan seasoning, blackened
- Italian Dressing
- 1 Steelhead, (a fillet)

Directions:

1. Preheat the grill to 350°F with a closed lid.
2. In an Iron: pan place the butter. Place the pan in the grill while preheating so that the butter melts. Coat the fillet with Italian dressing. Rub with Saskatchewan rub. Make sure the layer is thin. Mince the garlic and shallot. Remove the pan from the grill and add the garlic and shallots.

3. Spread the mixture on the fillet. Slice the lemon into slices. Place the slice on the butter mix.

4. Place the fish on the grate. Cook 20 - 30 minutes.

5. Remove from the grill and serve. Enjoy!

Nutrition: Calories: 230 Protein: 28g Carbs: 2g Fat: 14g

Grilled Sea Scallops with Corn Salad

Preparation Time: 25 minutes

Cooking Time: 30 minutes

Servings: 6

Ingredients:

- 6 shucked ears corn
- 1-pint grape tomatoes, halved
- 3 sliced scallions, white and light green parts only
- 1/3 cup basil leaves, finely shredded
- Salt and grounded pepper
- 1 small shallot, minced
- 2 tbsp. balsamic vinegar
- 2 tbsp. hot water
- 1 tsp. Dijon mustard ¼ cup
- 3 tbsp. sunflower oil
- 1 ½ pounds sea scallops

Intolerances:

- Gluten-Free
- Egg-Free
- Lactose-Free

Directions:

1. In a pot of boiling salted water, cook the corn for about 5 minutes. Drain and cool.

2. Place the corn into a big bowl and cut off the kernels. Add the tomatoes, scallions, and basil then season with salt and grounded pepper.

3. In a blender, mix the minced shallot with the vinegar, heated water, and mustard. With the blender on, gradually add 6 tbsp. of the sunflower oil.

4. Season the vinaigrette with salt and pepper; at that point, add it to the corn salad.

5. In a huge bowl, toss the remaining 1 tbsp. of oil with the scallops, then season with salt and grounded pepper.

6. Heat a grill pan. Put on half of the scallops and grill over high heat, turning once, until singed, around 4 minutes.

7. Repeat with the other half of the scallops. Place the corn salad on plates, then top with the scallops and serve.

Nutrition:

- Calories: 230
- Fat: 5g

- Cholesterol: 60mg
- Carbs: 13g
- Protein: 33g

Rub and Sauces Recipes

Smoked Garlic White Sauce

Preparation Time: 15 minutes

Cooking Time: 1 hour

Servings: 2

Ingredients:

- 2 cups hickory wood chips, soaked in water for 30 minutes
- 3 whole garlic heads
- ½ cup mayonnaise
- 1/3 cup sour cream
- 1 juiced lemon
- 2 tbsp. apple cider vinegar
- Salt to taste

Directions:

1. Cut garlic heads to expose the inside and place in a container, microwave-safe, with 2 tbsp. water. Microwave for about 5-6 minutes on medium.
2. Preheat your grill. Place garlic heads on a shallow foil "boat" and place it on the grill.

3. Close the grill and cook for about 20-25 minutes until soft completely. Remove and cool. Transfer into a blender then add the remaining ingredients. Process until smooth. Serve immediately or store in a refrigerator for up to 5 days.

Nutrition: Calories: 20 Fat: 0g Carbs: 8g Protein: 0g Fiber: 0g

Cheese and Breads

Grilled Peaches and Cream

Preparation Time: 15 minutes

Cooking Time: 8 minutes

Servings: 8

Ingredients:

- 4 halved and pitted peaches
- 1 tbsp. vegetable oil
- 2 tbsp. clover honey
- 1 cup cream cheese, soft with honey and nuts

Directions:

1. Preheat your Traeger grill to medium-high heat.
2. Coat the peaches lightly with oil and place on the grill pit side down.
3. Grill for about 5 minutes until nice grill marks on the surfaces.

4. Turn over the peaches then drizzle with honey.

5. Spread and cream cheese dollop where the pit was and grill for additional 2-3 minutes until the filling becomes warm.

6. Serve immediately.

Nutrition: Calories: 139 Fat: 10.2g Saturated Fat: 5g Carbs: 11.6g Net Carbs: 11.6g Protein: 1.1g Sugars: 12g Fiber: 0g Sodium: 135mg Potassium: 19mg

Rosemary Cheese Bread

Preparation Time: 10 minutes

Cooking Time: 12 minutes

Servings: 30 Breadstick

Ingredients:

- 1½ cup sunflower seeds
- ½ tsp. sea salt
- 1egg
- 1tsp. fresh rosemary (finely chopped)
- 2tsp. xanthan gum
- 2tbsp. cream cheese

- 2cups grated mozzarella

Directions:

1. Preheat the grill to 400°F with the lid closed for 15 minutes.
2. Toss the sunflower seeds into a powerful blender and blend until it smooth and flour-like.
3. Transfer the sunflower seed flour into a mixing bowl and add the rosemary and xanthan gum. Mix and set aside.
4. Melt the cheese in a microwave. To do this, combine the cream cheese and mozzarella cheese in a microwave-safe dish.
5. Place the microwave-safe dish in the grill and heat the cheese on high for 1 minute.
6. Bring out the dish and stir. Place the dish in the grill and heat for 30 seconds. Bring out the dish and stir until smooth.
7. Pour the melted cheese into a large mixing bowl.
8. Add the sunflower flour mixture to the melted cheese and stir the ingredients are well combined.
9. Add the salt and egg and mix thoroughly to form a smooth dough.

10. Measure out equal pieces of the dough and roll them into sticks.
11. Grease a baking sheet with oil and arrange the breadsticks into the baking sheet in a single layer.
12. Use the back of a knife or metal spoon to make lines on the breadsticks.
13. Place the baking sheet on the grill and make for about 12 minutes or until the breadsticks turn golden brown.
14. Remove the baking sheet from the grill and let the breadsticks cool for a few minutes.
15. Serve.

Nutrition:

- Calories: 23 Fat: 1.9 g
- Saturated Fat: 0.5 g
- Cholesterol: 7 mg
- Sodium: 47 mg
- Carbs: 0.6 g
- Fiber: 0.2 g
- Sugars: 0.1 g
- Protein: 1.2 g

Nut, Fruits and Dessert

Pineapple Cake

Preparation Time: 30 minutes

Cooking Time: 1 hour and 20 minutes

Servings: 8

Ingredients:

- 1 cup sugar
- 1 tbsp. baking powder
- 1 cup buttermilk
- ½ tsp. salt
- 1 jar maraschino cherries
- 1 stick butter, divided
- ¾ cup brown sugar
- 1 can pineapple slices
- 1 ½ cup flour

Directions:

1. Add Traegers to your smoker and follow your cooker's startup procedure. Preheat your smoker, with your lid closed, until it reaches 350.

2. Take a medium-sized cast Iron: skillet, melt one half stick butter. Be sure to coat the entire skillet. Sprinkle brown sugar into a cast Iron: skillet.

3. Lay the sliced pineapple on top of the brown sugar. Put a cherry into each individual pineapple ring.

4. Mix together the salt, baking powder, flour, and sugar. Add in the eggs, one-half stick melted butter and buttermilk. Whisk to combine.

5. Put the cake on the grill and cook for an hour.

6. Take off from the grill and let it sit for ten minutes. Flip onto a serving platter.

Nutrition:

- Calories: 120
- Protein: 1g
- Fiber: 0g
- Carbs: 18g
- Fat: 5g

Caramel Bananas

Preparation Time: 15 minutes

Cooking Time: 15 minutes Servings: 4

Ingredients:

- 1/3 cup chopped pecans
- ½ cup sweetened condensed milk
- 4 slightly green bananas
- ½ cup brown sugar
- 2 tbsp. corn syrup
- ½ cup butter

Directions:

1. Add Traeger to your smoker and follow your cooker's startup procedure. Preheat your smoker, with the lid closed, until it reaches 350.
2. Place the milk, corn syrup, butter, and brown sugar into a heavy saucepan and bring to boil. For five minutes, simmer the mixture on low heat. Stir frequently.
3. Place the bananas with their peels on, on the grill, and let them grill for five minutes. Flip and cook for five minutes more. Peels will be dark and might split.

4. Place on serving platter. Cut the ends off the bananas and split peel down the middle. Take the peel off the bananas and spoon caramel on top. Sprinkle with pecans.

Nutrition: Calories: 345 Protein: 11g Fiber: 3.1g Carbs: 77g Fat: 1g

Lamb Recipes

Traeger Smoked Leg

Preparation Time: 15 Minutes

Cooking Time: 3 Hours

Servings: 6

Ingredients:

- 1 leg lamb, boneless
- 2 tbsp. oil
- 4 garlic cloves, minced
- 2 tbsp. oregano
- 1 tbsp. thyme
- 2 tbsp. salt
- 1 tbsp. black pepper, freshly ground

Directions:

1. Trim excess fat from the lamb ensuring you keep the meat in an even thickness for even cooking.
2. In a mixing bowl, mix oil, garlic, and all spices. Rub the mixture all over the lamb then cover with a plastic wrap.
3. Place the lamb in a fridge and let marinate for an hour.
4. Transfer the lamb on a smoker rack and set the Traeger to smoke at 250°F.

5. Smoke the meat for 4 hours or until the internal temperature reaches 145°F.

6. Remove from the Traeger and serve immediately.

Nutrition:Calories: 356 Fat: 16g Carbs: 3g Protein: 49g Sugars: 1g Fiber: 1g odium: 2474mg

Traeger Smoked Lamb Meatballs

Preparation Time: 10 Minutes

Cooking Time: 1 Hour Servings: 20 Meatballs

Ingredients:

- 1 lb. lamb shoulder, ground
- 3 garlic cloves, finely diced
- 3 tbsp. shallot, diced
- 1 tbsp. salt
- 1 egg
- ½ tbsp. pepper
- ½ tbsp. cumin
- ½ tbsp. smoked paprika
- ¼ tbsp. red pepper flakes
- ¼ tbsp. cinnamon
- ¼ cup panko breadcrumbs

Directions:

1. Set your Traeger to 250°F.
2. Combine all the ingredients in a small bowl then mix thoroughly using your hands.

3. Form golf ball-sized meatballs and place them on a baking sheet. Place the baking sheet in the smoker and smoke until the internal temperature reaches 160°F.

4. Remove the meatballs from the smoker and serve when hot.

Nutrition:Calories: 93 Fat: 5.9g Carbs: 4.8g Protein: 5g Sugars: 0.3g Fiber: 0.3g Sodium: 174.1mg Potassium: 82.8mg

Traeger Crown Rack of Lamb

Preparation Time: 30 Minutes

Cooking Time: 30 Minutes

Servings: 6

Ingredients:

- 2 racks lamb. Frenched
- 1 tbsp. garlic, crushed
- 1 tbsp. rosemary
- ½ cup olive oil
- Kitchen twine

Directions:

1. Preheat your Traeger to 450°F.
2. Rinse the lab with clean cold water then pat it dry with a paper towel.
3. Lay the lamb flat on a chopping board and score a ¼ inch down between the bones. Repeat the process between the bones on each lamb rack. Set aside.
4. In a small mixing bowl, combine garlic, rosemary, and oil. Brush the lamb rack generously with the mixture.

5. Bend the lamb rack into a semicircle then place the frames together such that the bones will be up and will form a crown shape.

6. Wrap around 4 times starting from the base moving upward. Tie tightly to keep the racks together.

7. Place the lambs on a baking sheet and set them in the Traeger. Cook on high heat for 10 minutes. Reduce the temperature to 300°F and cook for 20 more minutes or until the internal temperature reaches 130°F.

8. Remove the lamb rack from the Traeger and let rest while wrapped in a foil for 15 minutes.

9. Serve when hot.

Nutrition:

- Calories: 390
- Fat: 35g
- Carbs: 0g
- Protein: 17g
- Sodium: 65mg

Appetizers and Sides

Roasted Cashews

Preparation Time: 15 Minutes

Cooking Time: 12 Minutes

Servings: 6

Ingredients:

- ¼ cup Rosemary, chopped
- 2 ½ tbsp. Butter, melted
- 2 cups Cashews, raw
- ½ tsp. Cayenne pepper
- 1 tsp. salt

Directions:

1. Preheat the grill to 350°F with a closed lid.
2. In a baking dish layer, the nuts. Combine the cayenne, salt rosemary, and butter. Add on top.
3. Grill for 12 minutes.
4. Serve and enjoy!

Nutrition:

- Calories: 150
- Protein: 5g
- Carbs: 7g

- Fat: 15g

Bacon BBQ Bites

Preparation Time: 10 Minutes

Cooking Time: 25 Minutes

Servings: 2 to 4

Ingredients:

- 1 tbsp. Fennel, ground
- ½ cup Brown Sugar
- 1 lb. Slab Bacon, cut into cubes (1 inch)
- 1 tsp. Black pepper
- Salt

Directions:

1. Take an aluminum foil and then fold in half.
2. Preheat the grill to 350°F with a closed lid.
3. In a bowl combine the black pepper, salt, fennel, and sugar. Stir.
4. Place the pork in the seasoning mixture. Toss to coat. Transfer on the foil.

5. Place the foil on the grill. Bake for 25 minutes, or until crispy and bubbly.

6. Serve and enjoy!

Nutrition:

- Calories: 300
- Protein: 27g
- Carbs: 4g
- Fat: 36g

Smoked Jerky

Preparation Time: 20 Minutes

Cooking Time: 6 Hours

Servings: 6 to 8

Ingredients:

- 1 Flank Steak (3lb.)
- ½ cup Brown Sugar
- 1 cup Bourbon
- ¼ cup Jerky rub
- 2 tbsp. Worcestershire sauce
- 1 can Chipotle
- ½ cup Cider Vinegar

Directions:

1. Slice the steak into ¼ inch slices.
2. Combine the remaining ingredients in a bowl. Stir well.
3. Place the steak in a plastic bag and add the marinade sauce. Marinade in the fridge overnight.
4. Preheat the grill to 180°F with a closed lid.
5. Remove the flank from the marinade. Place directly on a rack and on the grill.

6. Smoke for 6 hours.

7. Cover them lightly for 1 hour before serving. Store leftovers in the fridge.

Nutrition:Calories: 105 Protein: 14g Carbs: 4g Fat: 3g

Traditional Recipes

Bacon Wrapped Chicken Breasts

Preparation Time: 0 minute

Cooking Time: 3 hours

Servings: 6

Ingredients:

For Brine:

- ¼ cup brown Sugar:
- ¼ cup kosher salt
- 4 cups water

For Chicken:

- 6 skinless, boneless chicken breasts
- ¼ cup chicken rub
- 18 bacon slices
- 1½ cups BBQ sauce

Directions:

1. For the brine: in a large pitcher, dissolve Sugar: and salt in water.

2. Place the chicken breasts in brine and refrigerate for about 2 hours, flipping once in a middle way.

3. Preheat the Traeger grill & Smoker on grill setting to 230°F.

4. Remove chicken breasts from brine and rinse under cold running water.

5. Season chicken breasts with rub generously.

6. Arrange 3 bacon strips of bacon onto a cutting board, against each other.

7. Place 1 chicken breast across the bacon, leaving enough bacon on the left side to wrap it over just a little.

8. Wrap the bacon strips around the chicken breast and secure with toothpicks.

9. Repeat with remaining breasts and bacon slices.

10. Arrange the chicken breasts into a traeger grill and cook for about 2½ hours.

11. Coat the breasts with BBQ sauce and cook for about 30 minutes more.

12. Serve immediately.

Nutrition:

Calories: 481 Fat: 12.3 g

Saturated Fat: 4.2 g Cholesterol: 41 mg

Sodium: 3000 mg Carbs: 32 g

Fiber: 0.4g

Sugar: 22.2 g

Protein: 55.9 g

Sweet & Spicy Chicken Thighs

Preparation Time: 15 minutes Cooking Time: 15 minutes

Servings: 4

Ingredients:

- 2 garlic cloves, minced
- ¼ cup honey
- 2 tbsp. soy sauce
- ¼ tsp. red pepper flakes, crushed
- 4 (5-ounce) skinless, boneless chicken thighs
- 2 tbsp. olive oil
- 2 tsp. sweet rub

- ¼ tsp. red chili powder
- Ground black pepper, as required

Directions

1. Preheat the Traeger grill & Smoker on grill setting to 400°F.
2. In a small bowl, add garlic, honey, soy sauce, and red pepper flakes and with a wire whisk, beat until well combined.
3. Coat chicken thighs with oil and season with sweet rub, chili powder, and black pepper generously.
4. Arrange the chicken drumsticks onto the grill and cook for about 15 minutes per
5. In the last 4-5 minutes of cooking, coat drumsticks with garlic mixture. Serve immediately.

Nutrition:Calories: 309 Fat: 12.1 g Saturated Fat: 2.9 g Cholesterol: 82 mg Sodium: 504 mg Carbs: 18.7 g Fiber: 0.2 g Sugar 17.6 g Protein: 32.3 g

Lightning Source UK Ltd.
Milton Keynes UK
UKHW020631280521
384530UK00001B/156